The Mind Dancing

Tony Zurlo

Art and Calligraphy by Vivian Lu

Plain View Press
P. O. 42255
Austin, TX 78704

plainviewpress.net
sb@plainviewpress.net
512-441-2452

Copyright Tony Zurlo 2009. All rights reserved.
ISBN: 978-1-891386-26-8
Library of Congress Number: 2009921667

Dedication:

First of all, these poems are dedicated to my former students in China. By now, they are working and raising families. Their love and acceptance changed my life. Secondly, the collection is a tribute to that deeper, spiritual essence that has enabled China to survive and renew itself throughout history. Each poem and the entire collection is dedicated to my wife, Vivian Lu, whose inspiration and insight continue to refresh my own spirit and desire to work and write. Proof of her natural talent and enthusiasm for life are revealed in her graceful cover art, calligraphy, illustrations, and response poems in this collection.

Finally, this project would have been impossible without the idealism and patience of Susan Bright. I find her career and accomplishments at Plain View Press unrivaled because of her commitment to both subject and art while publishing an enthusiastic and talented group of artists and authors.

Tony Zurlo

Contents

An Art Form   7

Roots   9

    Dao: The Elusive One   11
    Dao: The Eternal One   12
    Chang E   13
    NOTES for Chang E   14
    Yin   17
    Household Disharmony   19
    The Stone's Secrets   21
    Still Without Rhyme   22
    Lao Zi   25
    The Buddha Waits   27
    Notes for The Buddha Waits   28
    Village Pageant   29
    Becoming One of the Immortals   30

Discovery   33

    Tracking Stillness   35
    Seek Virtue and the Spirits Will Follow   36
    Unbuilding Walls   39
    Mid Autumn Moon-Viewing   41
    Lip of the Sun   42
    Shadows on Beihai Lake   43
    Foreigner in the Street   44
    Foreigner in the Street   45
    The Visit   47
    Cultural Dust   48
    Souls of Ghosts   49
    Silent Jade   51
    For My Students   53
    Farewell   54
    A Cup of Wishes   56

Separation   57

    The Mind Dancing   59
    Preserving My Self   60
    Gifts   62
    Untamed Love   63
    Letter from my student in China   65
    A Simple Conversation   66
    Speechless Response   67
    Ink Stains on My Desk   68
    Waiting   71
    Letter from my wife   72
    Letter to my wife in China   73
    The Anarchy of Love   74

    Acknowledgments   75
    About the Poet and Artist   77

An Art Form

Chinese calligraphy is an abstract art form. Although it uses Chinese words as its vehicle of expression, one does not have to know Chinese to appreciate its beauty. Chinese calligraphy has many different kinds of writing styles. Like many Chinese, I practiced the formal or regular style of Chinese calligraphy when I was a little girl. As I grew up, I began to like Lishu (Clerical script) style and Semi-cursive script, because they look more artistic to me. The form of Lishu (Clerical) script was created by Cheng Miao in the Qin Dynasty.

When I first started to illustrate the poems, I wrote the Chinese characters in formal Lishu script, such as "Lip of the Sun" and in semi-cursive script like "Shadow Cloud." However, to Tony – an American without deep background knowledge about Chinese calligraphy, the formal Lishu style seems too rigid, and the brush strokes too thick and full. He appreciates the calligraphy's artistic beauty; in other words, he favors the movement of the strokes that run in a faster, freer style that suggests a dancing speed and a passion of life-force. Therefore, to express a beauty with rhythms of dancing speed, I have combined the Lishu style and Semi-cursive script together to write these Chinese characters for the poems.

In addition, I have kept the most noticeable stroke of the Lishu style for each character, which is the dramatically flared tail of one dominant horizontal stroke, especially that to the lower right. This characteristic stroke has famously been called "silkworm head and wild goose tail" (cántóu yànwěi) in Chinese due to its distinctive shape, which can be recognized in the characters of "Dance (wu)" in the title, "Confucius" (Kong lao fu zi), "Lao Zi," "Becoming One of the Immortals" – Love (ai), "Discovery" (xun), and "Tear Polished Jade" (lei guang-yu).

Vivian Lu

Roots

根

Dao (the Path or Way)

Dao: The Elusive One

consumes scholars
in missions of the mind,
convinced they can analyze
and split it like an atom,

attracts philosophers
like gravity, confident
they will tame it with
syllogisms and logic,

lures pilgrims to mountain tops,
guided by monks who promise
paradise to all who yield
to the scripture of bliss.

They litter the universe with
rumors and theories, then disappear
into the dark matter between stars,
the emptiness that is the cosmos.

Dao: The Eternal One

Dawn sheds her night clothes
and bathes in snow-melt brooks.
Blossoms perfume the air.

Buttered layers of sun
glaze fields with jellied primrose.
Sun sets, exhausted.

Frost paints meadows
with afterthoughts of summer.
Winter's sleep descends.

Chang E

A toast, Chang E.
Immortality you stole
from your husband's cup,
the tyrant King Hou Yi.
Now you know eternity.
And the gods have still
another Queen.

Old man Hou wanders
the jade-peaked mountains,
bow and arrow cocked,
waiting for your shadow.
He found immortality
shooting flaming arrows
across the night sky at you.

Slip into your Moon Palace,
Chang E, and tell me what
it's like to be the Queen
of Silence, another sacrifice
to appease the Heavens,
while the rose that waits
on earth drops another petal.

Chang E, come home.
Together we shall watch arrows
sketch desperate messages in the sky.
Together we shall crunch the moon
and count the years go by.
Together we shall tip the chalice
and melt the edges of eternity.

NOTES for Chang E

Title: A legendary Chinese queen who drank the King's elixir for immortality to save the people from his evil. The stories vary, but generally she was swept up into the sky, and her wish to visit the Moon Palace was immediately granted, except she never returned to Earth.

Stanza One: Hou Yi shot nine of ten suns out of the sky, thus saving the earth from disaster. He was made king by the people, but he lived a wanton life and became a murdering tyrant.

Stanza Two: The mountain of the fairy Queen Mother, Wang Mu, who gave the king the elixir. But Chang E stole it from him.

Stanza Four: The last two lines are a paraphrase from a poem by Song Dynasty poet Su Dongpo. Le, is the laughing, fat Buddha; Amitabha, the popular Buddha that saves all; Guanyin, the Goddess of Mercy with a thousand arms.

Chang E (Goddess of the Moon)

Yin

Yin

rules the night
from the shadows
of memory,

her words the waves
of creation, her voice
nature's lyre.

Through pristine air
she glides
undetected,

cradling the mystery
to her
bosom.

Confucius (Honorable, Respectful Scholar)

Household Disharmony

"If a man's self remains undeveloped, he is
incapable of guiding his family properly."
                    Kong Fu Zi (Confucius)

Dear Mr. Confucius:
How to develop my undeveloped Self,
Sir, is why I come to you for help.
I've analyzed ten thousand poems,
read the Classics, and practice the Golden Mean.
Was it as hard for you as seems to me?

My home I try to control, but my wife says
she's quite smart enough to think for herself.
She says men embellish their value to history,
because women, not men, preserve the society.
Name me one pure virtuous man, she screams.

And she interrupts my reply to credit your wife
for your worthy maxims. It's true, Confucius.
And your mother, she says, taught you everything.
That you could only prowl and growl when she
pulled you out of some tiger cave in the mountains.

There's no harmony in my household, Confucius.
My wife claims most of the world's wisdom
is feminine, and if I keep talking about Yin-Yang,
she's going to yin my yang. And she says you,
Confucius, are a Male Chauvinist Pig--

I tried to defend you, Confucius. Calmly, I said,
"Naturally, Sweetie Pie, but Confucius's mother
was only the 'Exalted *wife* of the King Who
Heralds the Sage,' his faithful, obedient wife
who knew her place in the scheme of life."

Well, all hell broke loose in my household,
like ten generations of angry ancestors
from her side of the family, my wife attacked
her "unworthy" husband. You can't imagine,
Confucius, life with the modern woman.

The next time I come, I expect to find you here.
After working like a slave to support my family
I go for some masculine advice, and you're out,
wandering the mountains dreaming up witty
one-liners. What kind of man are you, Confucius?

The Stone's Secrets

One foggy morning in late autumn
I missed the willow-walk to work
and cut across a hill where I discovered
an abandoned shrine shrouded in wild grasses,

the tips bowing toward untended gardens
with flowers scattered along a sycamore trail
that led back to the swelling in the earth
where a broad-shouldered block of stone—

with a hundred different secrets
chiseled by nature into its bone—
sat unobtrusively on this mound
a mystery scholars would unravel—

some day, but I hoped not soon
because I needed to believe that deep
inside their core, stones were strong
enough to keep secrets from me.

Still Without Rhyme

> "If one does not study poetry,
> one cannot express oneself."
> Kong Fu Zi (Confucius)

I visited the Confucius compound hoping for inspiration,
seeking poetic illumination. The honorable guide said,
"Master pre-busy cave thinking mountain over big river."

A man resembling the cypress tree planted 2,400 years ago
agreed to photographs—I wanted to capture that haze
of mystic poetry surrounding him for future inspiration.

An old woman stepped between us demanding cash, no plastic.
She collected, then he opened his royal robe wide, exposing
rows of Qufu Chamber of Commerce, Kiwanis, and Rotary pins.

I walked on, passing through Gates of this and that—
So many Gates to choose from I became disorientated
and flopped beneath a scholar tree to restore my senses.

Scant shade to think by, but I stared at the gnarled roots,
hoping for The Moment—My reason for coming, Master.
To learn from you how to live long and still be a spring poet.

The guide didn't understand why a foreign devil would worry
about rhyming Kiwanis with Confucius. "Confucius say:
'Guide rhymes with died'," I warned. "So shut up and guide."

He said he had to go relieve himself, so I resumed on my own,
desperate for rhythm and rhyme, passing through many gates
before stumbling upon the "Gate of Augmenting the Truth."

Impatient, I stopped to read inscriptions on the gate: "Li loves
Wang," "Liu loves Li," "Zhou loves Wei Wei," "Liu loves Zhou
and Wei Wei," "Wang loves Liu and Zhou," Wei Wei loves . . . ."

I tossed my English–Chinese dictionary into a pond and circled
back and forth. Passed through the "Gate of the Great Mean"
but missed the "Wall of Lu"—the Concealing Books Wall.

I cornered an official and complained about the honorable guide.
He told me to buy some Qufu Lions Club pennants and be happy.
I sat under a chestnut tree and massaged a Panda-sized headache.

At day's end I boarded the bus without rhyme or rhythm, resolved
to return. I'd skip the guides and gates and corner Confucius at
his favorite hideout: the cave thinking mountain over big river.

Lao Zi

Lao Zi

"The name that can be named
is not the eternal name."

Lao Zi wasn't his real name.
Like the Dao he claimed no name
      and every name.

"A hundred schools contended"
over the nature of human nature.
  Good or bad?

Their battles destroyed careers,
as sages debunked each others' view
  as unnatural.

Every thinker in the land
had a theory, and every theory
  had a name.

Except for Lao Zi's. He proposed
that naming was a disguise
  for ignorance.

Lao Zi had little else to say,
so he bowed and retreated
  to the mountains.

A guard asked for his passport.
Lao Zi asked for a brush, ink,
  stone, and paper.

He sat on the ground and with
quick strokes he wrote out
  essential lyrics.

Leaving his poems with the guard,
Lao Zi disappeared through the pass
   forever.

For centuries now, they've studied
his passport for clues of his
   location.

They've probed the dense forests,
examined the pebbles in streams,
   but his trail

Has led to everywhere and to
nowhere, his destination
   unknown.

The Buddha Waits

(Meditations on Spring at Longxing Temple)

Mi Le's belly bounces when he greets them.
Amitabha watches serenely as they walk.
Guanyin extends abundant arms to guide them
One thousand sitting Buddhas chant.

Beside a clay wall, bees nurse on cherry trees
with butterfly-blossoms quivering in the breeze.
Two sparrows loiter in mid air, circling tongues of grass,
dip left-then right, perchance a lovers' dance.

Doves settle in the rafters, a sultry breeze slips in
and fondles her black hair, then disappears,
leaving a scent of jasmine and plowed soil.
He closes his blue eyes to see:

Journeying back beneath snow clouds;
holding hands under a red canopy of maple leaves;
back further to lips like lotus blossoms;
into the folds of velvet petals he disappears.

He joins his palms in reverence,
but feels her breath warming his ear—
sweet and saucy secrets caught in mid-flight.
What will the Buddha do?

Mi Le's belly bounces
Amitabha watches serenely
Guanyin extends abundant arms
A thousand chanting Buddhas wait.

NOTES for The Buddha Waits

Longxing Temple in Zhengding, P.R. China, was built in 586 A.D., in the reign of Kaihuang, Sui Dynasty.

The thousand Buddhas are on the statue of the bronze Vairocana, with 1,072 figures of Buddha on three layers, four larger Buddhas at each layer, back to back facing the four directions, and then tiny ones carved below each.

Village Pageant

Peasants bob like chickens
pecking at the stubborn ground.
A boy with bamboo arms beckons
a donkey and a reluctant hound.

Garments loiter all day
like ghosts with lethargic eyes.
Children tease each other at play
while elders comfort babies' cries.

Along a loess-dusted road a generation
of women stroll, each voice an instrument
from the past, each step a celebration
of an ageless Chinese village pageant.

Becoming One of the Immortals

I Ching scholars and Tai Chi masters,
Taiji sages and Feng Shui monks—
From the four corners they came
to meet in the mist at Mount Tai
to solve the mystery of living right.

The mist grew heavy on the mountain top
while the kingdom's exalted thinkers mulled
over shifting views: "Confucius argued this..."
"Lao Zi claimed that..." "The Buddha believed...?"
Yin and Yang spinning freely on the Mount.

Far beneath the heavenly peak, unaware
of major deviations or revisions in nature's laws,
peasants worked their rice paddies and patched
leaks in their houses; after supper they convened
under torch light to repair the village granary.

After repairs they gathered late beneath the sky.
With weary arms they passed around the wine skin,
offering thanks to their ancestors for a good day
and asking for plentiful crops and family health.
The mountain mist drifting out to sea.

Ai (Love)

Discovery

Tracking Stillness

Above rain-soaked plains
pilgrims trek up hillside paths.
Jade-veined mountain peaks

Seekers of stillness
listen to whispering streams.
Trees color-coded.

Winter digests doubts.
Spring dew teases open
lips of peonies.

Seek Virtue and the Spirits Will Follow

I cloistered myself
above the Yangzi
to seek virtue,

the character with a foot
pursuing truth,
supported by a heart.

Pacing the forest floor,
in angled light I called
on Lao Zi for a clue.

"The wise man
...disregards himself,
and his Self is increased.

"He gives himself away
and his Self is preserved."
So, I disregarded myself.

I watched a river of boats,
fishermen tossing nets,
oxen pulling plows.

I already knew these
to be the way of things,
the outcomes, but of what?

On the ninth day
from inside chamber walls,
I heard voices,

a congress convened
on essences, a council
of non-beings.

"Observe the bamboo
in the wind" one
shadow instructed.

Another insisted,
"Be the bamboo
in the wind."

I took one step
and one shadow followed,
another step~another

followed. I twirled
and they all twirled,
and the wall moved.

The Great Wall

Unbuilding Walls

In summer, I arrived
at the Great Wall,
confident that a pile
of stones could never
block my path, convinced
my will would overcome.

So I circled circles
and circled around,
leaving ten thousand
footprints along the wall
that disappeared in the fall
beneath wind-blown dunes.

Ten thousand thousand
grains I tossed that fall,
and still so much wall
remained, an endless
trail of stones unclaimed,
I began to doubt.

Fleeing into the winter,
I gathered stone to build
my own fortification,
measuring carefully
each angle, leveling
and testing each layer.

I reinforced against
the north wind and erected
a snow fence to the west.
And each morning armed,
I marched out to inspect
my private wall for breaks.

Spring thaw cracked a corner,
and I watched a China rose
slip through, then another corner
cracked and let another in,
and an army of roses invaded
and overran my wall.

Mid Autumn Moon-Viewing

Mid-Autumn's moon
   hides behind
   night mist.
But keep watch--

A smile will clear
   a passageway
   to the corner
I've reserved for you.

Lip of the Sun

"Bright colors are unnatural
for most of us," you claim,
lowering your midnight eyes
in modesty. "We Han people
are naturally reserved."

I may never know the mysteries
your eyes conceal, secrets
embedded in creases of history.
But I know the brilliance
of your face that lights my days.

Its radiance rides waves
across the horizon, and gathers in
the melting sun, and encircles me
with golden arms glowing,
offering me the lip of the sun.

Shadows on Beihai Lake

Behind scaffolds the Buddha sleeps,
while shadows glide across the water
parting lotus leaves in their paths,
struggling against the current,
wings fully extended, circling
like swans in pas de deux,
or the firebird in defiant dance.

Couples climb the Buddha hill,
hand in hand, armed with cameras.
But none know the brilliance
of nature's will to curl East
and West around the twirling sun.

Beneath the "Cloudy and Shady Bridge"
yin and yang converge.

Foreigner in the Street

(*by* Vivian Lu)

I saw a foreigner in the street in China.
His skin color stood out from the rest
highlighting our differences.
A high forehead and big nose
shaded mysteries that lured me.
Green-bluish eyes sheltered his thoughts
my wild imagination begged to hear.

I'd been passing by him for years
exploring those eyes, and finally
found the same sky and sea of blue,
the same grasses swaying in the field
and the forest ever greens.

The shaded mysteries unfolded
and I discovered the same ego and dream in him
that I have had all of my life, too.
I no longer see him as a foreigner in the street.

Foreigner in the Street

(Tony's Response Poem)

He is a foreigner, she knows
not from his casual dress or height,
but his large egg-shaped eyes,
green like lazy lotus leaves.
And when they shift to look at her,
the blue sky frames his tanned face.

She knows because his nose is long
and angular and flared like a stallion.
His hair is bleached-out brown
from too many hours under the sun,
and his hips sway with a western rhythm,
a swagger unlike any Asian gait.

From him radiates an energy for being,
an offer to seek the universe squeezed
into a shell and turn customs upside down,
to walk defiantly through Tiananmen
and shout nonsense at officialdom,
to feel the passion that awakens life.

Bai Fang (Gracious Visit)

The Visit

"Like refrigerator outside"–
Your words a melody of Chinese tones
accented with eyes that hesitate
a pivot away from flight.

"Like warm stove inside"–
A thought caught loitering half way
between my throat and lips,
tumbling out of rhythm, out of tune.

Before I ask, you offer apologies:
the person I expected was called away–
Nonsense syllables to divert me
from the poetry of your eyes.

From those I read deeply and reach out
to touch the soul that guides them,
eyes wide like "lotus leaves dancing
in the chaos" of "the white wave."

Such courage you show to even ask
"Should I visit?" And then your surprise:
a half-smile, but unspoken: "Do I dare?"
And the lotus leaves rehearse their next step.

Cultural Dust

Fog muted the wistful wind
rattling my windowpane.
And slipping into my room
was not you, but dreams of you

or rather the ghost of you
hiding in dream's shadows,
eluding your ancestors' taboos,
their sacred racial canons—

Where is the bold Asian adventurer
who exploded into my imagination
one midnight past riding the bucking wind
across the great wall with delirious passion,

shattering stone tablets into archeological
rubble with such primordial power that desert
sands fused into ten thousand glass panes
reflecting the original plans of Heaven.

Souls of Ghosts

Last night I dreamed a visit
from a golden-hued princess
who shared secrets as ancient
and fresh as Nature's Soul.

Secrets so fundamental and simple
that scholars and priests ignore
these views as too primitive
for today's complicated world.

Fingers tracing wrinkles on my cheek,
hair tickling my neck. These curled
my senses and awakened dervishes
whirling me back to the beginning.

One night soon, my golden Muse,
the Soul of this foreign ghost
will enter your room and whisper
words fit for the origin of things.

洞光玉

Lei Guang Yu (Tear Polished Jade)

Silent Jade

Pale jade in the corner, overcast
eyes swollen like the gloomy sky
pregnant with storm, what at last
reduced your June-Fourth will to defy?

What extinguished the blaze that curled
the lives that whirled around you?
What power diminished your glow and hurled
dizzy dreams away and turned you blue?

My tongue numb, the philosopher's enigma,
my windy promises deflated by clichés,
my smile clinging to memory in this dilemma.
I have delayed descent into madness for days

To touch your hand just one more time.
I reach out but a dozen hands grab mine.

Willow Walk

For My Students

Young willow arms wave
Old sycamores moan

I walk to the stone sitting
like Mi Le among the trees

Rubbing the stone's smooth belly
I make one final wish~

"They've sacrificed and suffered much
so leave them their dignity"

I wait for a sign~It's not by faith
alone. . . We're promised a sign

But the stone wears its usual face
age-lines etched by time

Scar tissue falls from sycamores
as their stiff bones bend

Willow arms sway left then right
checking the way of the wind.

"Foolish old man," I scold and walk away,
leaving my wishes behind

Mi Le is the chubby, smiling Buddha who helps people with their wishes.

Farewell

We never tipped a pot of wine
nor wondered when the moon
first climbed the sky.
We never swam the Silver River
to spy from the bridge of magpies.

As autumn sets, the sun
bleeds freely, and I sit
beneath shadowy pines,
recalling the night we debated
one of Li Bai's famous lines.

Into an ink-stained landscape
I slip, fog-shrouded valleys dip
between crimson mountains, and I ride
rainbows to the edge of the world
where the four winds collide.

I start in opposite directions,
split images under a stone bridge,
drifting apart on wooden rafts
seeking the unknowable, sailing
with wine cups lifted to the wind.

Line 1 refers to Li Bai's "Drinking Alone by Moonlight": ~
"Among the flowers a pot of wine, / I drink alone; no friend is by."

Line 3 refers to Li Bai's "Reflections on the Moon While Drinking": ~
"When did the moon first appear in the sky?"

Line 4 refers to the Milky Way. In the legend of the Cowherd and Weaving Maid, they loved each other so deeply that the phoenix called all the magpies in the universe to link together to form a bridge so the couple could cross to see each other one night a year (seventh day of the seventh month).

A Cup of Wishes

I imagine you walking home at night,
staring into the windows of my old room,
lured by the gravity of emptiness.
The breeze fingers wild curls in your hair.
In the dark, forest tongues whisper:
"When phantoms roam, owls blink,
nightingales disguise their voices,
narcissus mark the trail to silence...."

Phantoms, owls, nightingales, flowers~
none are important signs for this hour.
At this very moment I am collecting my wishes
in the cup of my hands and blowing them free,
each wish a special sonnet for Lady Night
to sing to you while you sleep.

Lady Night refers to erotically suggestive songs popular especially in southern China during the Six Dynasty period, 300-600 AD. A mysterious woman known as "Lady Night" or "Midnight" is believed to have written and sung the first group of these songs.

Separation

The Mind Dancing

To love China is to love not
    the thing itself,
    but the idea of loving,
    and never knowing.

Lovers will forever be charred
    by the Dragon~
    ashes into dust,
  yellow earth.

Born in turmoil and nurtured
    in mystery, China
    leaves a vapor trail
    of newborn stars.

China reveals itself
    to no one~
    China is the
    mind dancing.

Preserving My Self

(The Wise Man "...disregards himself,
and his Self is increased. He gives
himself away and his Self is preserved."
                    Lao Zi)

I: The Wisdom of the East

Seeking the wisdom of Asia, I secluded my Self
in mountains with air so thin I could hear orations
explicating meanings of life. Seek the Self. Destroy
the Self: "To Be or Not To Be" run rampant.

A voice I named the Dark Side chanted simply,
"Follow the wind." To the north I dashed—straight
into a granite wall; to the south, another; and the wind
shifted again: east then west; north and south.

Exhausted, I retreated into the mouth of a cave.
A new voice, I called the Gray Side, inflated the air within:
"Go with the flow. Chill out, dude. Catch the cosmic vibes.
Love and Peace, brother. Get with the groove. You dig?"

Choking on indigestible cave philosophy, I thought aloud:
The rhythm's not comfortable. Maybe it's the translation.
I needed a third opinion to bring Lao Zi's meaning to light,
so I left the cave for the cliffs and a breathe of fresh air.

More voices drifted across the abyss and pitched tent
on my rock. A non-stop harangue: "Hang 'em high."
"Put 'em in irons." "Throw away the keys." Reminded
me of a few friends of mine, but not Lao Zi.

II: The Wisdom of the West

I decided to leave the rock, the cave, and the mountain top.
Back home in familiar surroundings, I watched shows about
life and death, reruns of Bruce Lee, Jet Li, and Jackie Chan.
Like Lao Zi, they all said I must give my Self away.

For the sake of preserving my disregarded self I listened
carefully everyday: "...one life to live, so live it with gusto."
"Be all that you can be," "We really move our tail for you."
So many wise voices on the talking box can be confusing.

I watched a soft voice speaking in surround-sound. It was
Trixie holding a blackberry or raspberry phone hip-high.
Said something about being in her Fave Five for wisdom
that will curl my toes if I will give my self away tonight.

Gifts

Wherever I take my days
I carry your laughter
to disperse the clouds
that wrap themselves around me
and wear your smile on my vest
to chase away the raging storms.

When evening folds up its edges
to the corners of my room
I spread your gifts across my bed
and touch each one with moonlight
before I tuck myself beneath them
to wait for Midnight~

Thoughts stalk empty space.
Dawn winks in the Eastern Sky.

Erotically suggestive songs were popular especially in southern China during the Six Dynasty period, 300-600 A.D. A mysterious woman known as "Midnight" (and "Lady Night") is believed to have written and sung the first group of these songs.

Untamed Love

She enticed me with no promises
that we'd seize eternity,
no silence, no peace—

Defiance, insubordination,
hostilities with the gods was her offer
if I agreed—

a perilous love,
boldly dismissing those who enclosed us
in the cultural swill,

a soaring love
that only the insane dare ride
into the void of galaxies.

With untamed love our armament,
we stormed the membrane
of the universe.

Chang Le (Happiness Forever)

Letter from my student in China

What shall I say now that you're not here?
Why do I see your face looking up at me
from my writing desk?

How could I become friends with someone
who always thinks of me as a little girl?
I do not know why?

Every time I talk about you I keep a happy face.
When I tell my parents they just smile
as if they know some secret.

My grandpa broke up laughing when I told him
about teaching you your name in Chinese:
"Mudhead, that's me," you said.

How deeply thankful I was. Because of you
I could bring my respectful grandfather
one last happy weekend.

A Simple Conversation

I talk to you everyday—
a simple conversation
about roses and gardens
dandelions in grass

should we plant wild flowers
on the hill? run ivy up the stairs?
how to protect our China Doll
from winter's freeze?

a few words each day
flung into turbulent air
casual thoughts expressed
by nature's breath

I hold up half the sky
while waiting into the nighttime
of our lives, apart~
endless oceans apart

I marvel at our lives
and wonder about eternity
and supporting half of heaven~
will there be time for simple talk?

Speechless Response

by Vivian Lu

The voice of your simple conversation
travels faster than light
Just in a second
it echoes in my mind

My answer is the tears of two rivers-
the Yellow River and the Yangzi River
with a silent sound of singing water
'Cause I am speechless in response

Ink Stains on My Desk

I retreated into my study
to read the latest from Xanadu.
Her words tumbled onto my desk,
staining the mahogany finish:
"Dear husband, I feel shame that I failed
to introduce you to my parents."

From across the peaceful sea, she wrote:
"Sorry that this is a forbidden marriage.
I only introduced my 'yang-gui-zi' dog
to my relatives. My white, 'yang-gui-zi'
husband whom I love so much
is an outsider in my land."

I drew my words carefully from
the ink stains on my desk:
"Your 'foreign devil' husband
raises his pitchfork in response.
It matters not what yellow people think
nor white nor black nor brown.

"What are colors but the gods' way
of displaying the wonders of the world.
Some days I'm a dazzling red, others
an overcast gray. What color are you
today? Green or yellow, striped or speckled,
you're the end of the rainbow for me."

Absence

陰陽扣隔

Yi Yang Xiang Ge (Yin and Yang Apart)

Waiting

Once flushed peach blossoms
wilt ten thousand li from me.
Crows circle above.

Flowers in spring snow.
Fruit on a distant hilltop
on gnarled limbs.

Shadows dip then drift,
teasing memories of you.
Will my moon return?

Letter from my wife

When I was a little girl in China,
I worried about the danger and death
that might happen to my mom and dad,
so I told them that I would stop eating;
that way, I would not grow up
and then they would never grow old.

Then I forgot all about death,
just a glancing thought sometimes.
I ate a lot and grew up forgetting
about my promise to mom and dad,
until I was in my thirties and suddenly
noticed some gray in mom's hair.

Then I got a job in America, and every day
the news reports about death: people my age
dead from strokes and heart attacks and cancer,
young mothers killing babies and the young
killing the young, hikers lost in mountains,
tsunamis, Katrina, suicide bombers—Darfu.

When I think about mom and dad, I want
to laugh with them about my little-girl promise,
to grab them and cling to them, to thank them
for living long and staying healthy, and I want
to tell them about the loves of my life, and how much
I fear death, but I have to squeeze back tears instead.

But they are happy. They live to enjoy the time left
together, day-to-day, hour-by-hour. On my last visit
I bought my dad a new tool set, and he plays Mr. Fixit;
and my mom a MP3, and she records her favorite Tang
and Song poems. When it was time to leave, though,
they suddenly were old and begged me to stay forever.

Letter to my wife in China

I wrote the perfect story
with an ending that never ends:
Hawaiian surf and Polynesian sun.
Beautiful daughters, handsome sons,

We live forever in fairy tales.

I bought holiday lights for the cypress.
Their tiny stars twinkling can be seen
for miles along the highway, our secret
each midnight hitching a ride to China.

Fairy tales never ending.

The Anarchy of Love

To know her better,
is to know her less,
each day an invitation
into turmoil, each week
a temptation into chaos.

Exploring different threads
of her quilted character,
I uncover an uncharted world
and soar like a whirling dervish,
addicted to intrigue and suspense.

Enchanted by her mystery—
Lost in the bedlam of love—
I release, yielding and embracing
the endless universes of madness,
and together we explore anarchy.

Acknowledgments

"The Anarchy of Love," *AIAP (All Info About Poetry)*, Issue 113, June 23, 2006, <http://www,allinfoaboutpoetry,com/sitemap,html>; "The Buddha Waits," *New Texas* 2005; "Chang E," *open windows: the online anthology of Texas poetry*, 2006, <http://www,english,tamu,edu/cw/owp/>; "Cultural Dust," Golden Apple Press (1997); "A Cup of Wishes," *The Sunday Suitor Poetry Journal* 9, April 1998; "Dao: The Elusive One," *Long Story Short* 7, March 2007, <http://www,alongstoryshort,net/>, *In These Latitudes: Ten Contemporary Poets*, Ed, Robert Bonazzi, San Antonio: Wings Press, 2008; "Dao: The Eternal One," *Long Story Short* 7 March 2007, <http://www,alongstoryshort,net/>; *In These Latitudes: Ten Contemporary Poets*, Ed, Robert Bonazzi, San Antonio: Wings Press, 2008; "Farewell," *Identity Theory*, Winter 2005-06, <http://www,identitytheory,com/verse/dec_2005,php>; "A Foreigner in the Street," *River Walk Journal* 3,4, Nov, Dec, 2006; <http://www,riverwalkjournal,org/riverwalkjournal3-4,pdf>; "Gifts," *The Sunday Suitor Poetry Journal*, August 1997; "Household Disharmony," *Fickle Muses*, March 4-10, 2007, <http://www,ficklemuses,com/index,html>; "Ink Stains on My Desk," *AIAP*, Issue 116, March 3, 2007, <http://www,allinfoaboutpoetry,com/news116,html>, In These Latitudes: Ten Contemporary Poets, Ed, Robert Bonazzi, San Antonio: Wings Press, 2008; "Lao Zi," *RPCV Writers & Readers* 8,2, March 1996, *In These Latitudes: Ten Contemporary Poets*, Ed, Robert Bonazzi, San Antonio: Wings Press, 2008; "For My Students,"[Published as "The Last Walk," *Möbius*, 1996; "The Lip of the Sun," *Möbius* 1996; "Mid Autumn Moon Viewing," *Orphic Lute* 41,1, Spring 1991; "Mind Dancing," *In These Latitudes: Ten Contemporary Poets*, Ed, Robert Bonazzi, San Antonio: Wings Press, 2008; "Shadows on Beihai Lake," Snow Monkey 6,2 (2004), *In These Latitudes: Ten Contemporary Poets*, Ed, Robert Bonazzi, San Antonio: Wings Press, 2008; "Silent Jade," *The Sunday Suitor Poetry Journal*, October 1998; "A Simple Conversation," *New Texas* 2001, In These Latitudes: Ten Contemporary Poets, Ed, Robert Bonazzi, San Antonio: Wings Press, 2008; "Souls of Ghosts," *In These Latitudes: Ten Contemporary Poets*, Ed, Robert Bonazzi, San Antonio: Wings Pres, 2008; "Still Without Rhyme," *Fickle Muses*,

March 4-10, 2007, <http://www,ficklemuses,com/index,html>; "Unbuilding Walls," *The Sunday Suitor Poetry Journal* 10, June 1998, *In These Latitudes: Ten Contemporary Poets*, Ed, Robert Bonazzi, San Antonio: Wings Press, 2008; "Untamed Love," *New Texas* 2002, *In These Latitudes: Ten Contemporary Poets*, Ed, Robert Bonazzi, San Antonio: Wings Press, 2008; "Village Pageant," *In These Latitudes: Ten Contemporary Poets*, Ed, Robert Bonazzi, San Antonio: Wings Press, 2008; "The Visit," *DiVerseCity Anthology*, Austin: Austin Poets International Inc,, 2003, *In These Latitudes: Ten Contemporary Poets*, Ed, Robert Bonazzi, San Antonio: Wings Press, 2008; "Waiting," *In These Latitudes: Ten Contemporary Poets*, Ed, Robert Bonazzi, San Antonio: Wings Press, 2008; "Yin," *The Word: The Monthly Guide to the Arts in Dallas* (TX), (August 1995), *In These Latitudes: Ten Contemporary Poets*, Ed, Robert Bonazzi, San Antonio: Wings Press, 2008;

About the Poet and Artist

Tony Zurlo'spoetry and fiction have appeared more than one hundred print and online journals. His newest publications include twelve poems in the anthology edited by Robert Bonazzi titled *In These Latitudes: Ten Contemporary Poets*. San Antonio: Wings Press, 2008 and "Marco's Marcoroni," a short story in the anthology, *Wild Dreams: The Best of Italian Americana*. NY: Fordham University Press, 2008.

Zurlo has published books on Vietnam, China, Hong Kong, Japan, Japanese Americans, West Africa, Algeria, Syria, and the United States Congress. His Op-eds and reviews have appeared in many newspapers and journals, such as the *Houston Chronicle*, the *Fort Worth Star-Telegram*, *Online Journal*, *Dissident Voice*, *Peace Corps Writers*, *Democrats.US*, *The Externalist*, *Populist America*, *Red River Review*, *River Walk Journal*, *Clockwise Cat*, *Armageddon Buffet*, *Fickle Muses*, and *The November 3rd Club*, among others.

Vivian Lu has worked for many years as an educator in China and Texas. She returns annually to China as a guest lecturer in her home city. Vivian has displayed her artwork, including origami scenes from the Chinese classic *Journey to the West* throughout Dallas and Ft. Worth. She has published poetry in *New Texas* 2001, and has read her poetry at the Austin International Poetry Festival.

Besides working full time at Tarrant County College, Vivian is active in tutoring English and teaching Chinese to children in the metroplex.

www.ingramcontent.com/pod-product-compliance
Lightning Source LLC
Chambersburg PA
CBHW071031080526
44587CB00015B/2568